U.S. NAVY

JEN BESEL

BLACK RABBIT BOOKS

Bolt Jr. is published by Black Rabbit Books
P.O. Box 227, Mankato, Minnesota, 56002
www.blackrabbitbooks.com

Michael Sellner, designer and photo researcher

Library of Congress Cataloging-in-Publication Data is on file with the Library of Congress

Library Binding ISBN: 9781623107642
Paperback ISBN: 9781644665916
eBook ISBN: 9781623107703

LCCN: 2022933432

Image Credits

Alamy: ABFootage, 6; AB Forces News Collection, 12; MC2 Alex Perlman/U.S. Navy, 20–21; PJF Military Collection, 18–19, 23; Stocktrek Images, Inc., 11; Dreamstime: Razihusin, 1; Getty: Stocktrek Images, 8–9; Shutterstock: Beautiful landscape, 10; Dzmitry Kim, 3, 24; PHOTOOBJECT, 21; vadimmmus, 14–15; U.S. Air Force: Lt Col Leslie Pratt, 13; US Air Force Master Sergeant John Nimmo, 4; U.S. Navy: MCC Shannon Renfroe, Cover; USNI News, 16–17; Wikimedia Commons: Andy Wolfe/U.S. Navy, 4–5

Contents

CHAPTER 1

What Is the U.S. Navy?

The **aircraft carrier** bounces in the waves. A jet flies toward it. Navy sailors on the ship get ready. The jet is going to land on the ship.

aircraft carrier: a warship on which aircraft can be launched and landed

Mr. Elliot "Hemo" Clemence
75
RESCUE
VX-23
USS NIMITZ
Crew Chief Michael Devine
FTCE Kenneth Glass
NAVY

Soldiers at Sea

The Navy is part of the U.S. military. Members work on ships. Others fly planes. They help keep the United States safe.

COMPARING NAVY SHIPS

aircraft carriers
1,092 feet (333 meters) long

destroyers
about 500 feet
(152 m) long

PARTS OF AN Aircraft Carrier

island
runways

CHAPTER 2

Training

New sailors have a lot to learn. They start with **basic training**. They become strong swimmers. They learn to use weapons.

basic training: the first few weeks of learning for someone who has joined the military

FACT
Basic training lasts about eight weeks.

On the Job

After basic training, sailors have more school. Some learn to fix ships. Others become pilots. Some even fly **drones**.

drone: an unmanned aircraft or ship guided by a remote control or computer

U.S. Navy Bases

Asia
Europe
Africa
Australia

CHAPTER 3

Ships and Subs

The Navy uses many ships. Destroyers have weapons to fight enemies. Jets launch and land from aircraft carriers at sea.

FACT
More than 5,000 people travel on a carrier.

Subs

The Navy uses submarines for secret jobs. Subs fire weapons underwater. They attack enemies.

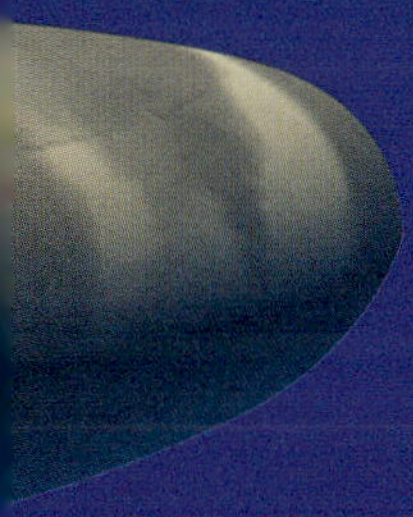

How Deep an Ohio Class Sub Can Dive

more than 800 feet (244 m) deep

Bonus Facts

Subs can stay underwater for months.

The Navy has more than 330,000 members.

The U.S. Navy started in 1775.

Six U.S. **presidents** were sailors.

president: the head of the government in some countries

READ MORE/WEBSITES

Billings, Tanner. *The U.S. Navy.* Inside the U.S. Military. New York: Rosen Publishing, 2022.

Miller, Marie-Therese. *The U.S. Navy in Action.* U.S. Military Branches. Minneapolis: Lerner Publications, 2023.

Morey, Allan. *U.S. Navy.* U.S. Armed Forces. Minneapolis: Jump!, Inc., 2021.

America's Navy—YouTube
www.youtube.com/c/americasnavy/featured

United States Navy
www.navy.mil/

503

GLOSSARY

aircraft carrier (AYR-kraft KAR-ee-uhr)—a warship on which aircraft can be launched and landed

basic training (BAY-sik TRAYN-ing)—the first few weeks of learning for someone who has joined the military

drone (DROHN)—an unmanned aircraft or ship guided by a remote control or computer

president (PREZ-uh-dent)—the head of the government in some countries

INDEX